Welcome to My World

FOOD
Around the World

by Ellen Lawrence

Ruby Tuesday Books

Published in 2026 by Ruby Tuesday Books Ltd.

Editor: Mark J. Sachner
Design & Production: Tammy West

Photo credits:
Alamy: 4L (Jorge Fernandez), 4C (E.D. Torial), 9 (Sourcenext), 17 (Wayne Tippetts), 19L (World Religions Photo Library), 21 (Westend61 GmbH); Corbis: 19R; FLPA: 5L, 5T, 12–13, 15; Shutterstock: Cover (Connect Images-Curated), 4R (Tom Wang), 5BR (ribeiroantonio), 6L (Anurak Pongpatimet), 6R (Elena Veselova), 7T (swissmacky), 7, 8L (Galliina), 8R (Usako), 10 (knot9images), 11 (Arisha Ray Singh), 14L, 14R (Claudio Zaccherini), 16 (Alex Yeung/stocksolutions/Fanfo/Icswart/Yeti studio), 18 (margouillat photo), 20 (africa924), 24 (Galiina).

Library of Congress Control Number: 2024948738
Hardback ISBN 978-1-78856-540-0
Paperback ISBN 978-1-78856-541-7
ePub ISBN 978-1-78856-542-4

Published in Minneapolis, MN
Printed in the United States

www.rubytuesdaybooks.com

The picture on the front cover of this book shows boys in Sweden enjoying pizza after a soccer game.

CONTENTS

Let's Eat! 4
A Worldwide Food 6
Funny Food Faces 8
Homemade Diwali Sweets 10
Hunting and Gathering 12
Yak Meat and Milk 14
A Fish Supper 16
Together for Iftar 18
Not Enough Food to Eat 20
Welcome to My World 22
Glossary 23
Index 24

Words shown in bold in the text are explained in the glossary.

All the places in this book are shown on the map on page 22.

Let's Eat!

It's porridge for breakfast in Namibia.

A school lunch of sausage and fries in Germany.

A delicious dinner of noodles in the United States.

This family in Rwanda grows the vegetables they eat in their own garden.

Fruit is a popular food all over the world.

Durian fruit

In Malaysia, many people eat durian fruit. The flesh of this fruit tastes like a mixture of custard, onions, and cheese. In Mexico, people eat black sapote fruit, which tastes like chocolate!

Black sapote fruit

A Worldwide Food

There is one food that people eat all over the world—rice.

Rice grains

Rice is a type of grass plant.

The rice grains we eat are the plant's seeds.

People grow and eat more than 40,000 different types of rice!

Halloween treats made from puffed rice cereal

A farmer planting rice plants

Rice plants grow best in places where the land is very wet. Often farmers flood their rice fields with water from nearby rivers. In some places, farmers use water buffaloes to **plow** the wet, muddy fields before the rice is planted.

Farmers plowing the flooded fields with water buffaloes

Rice growing in flooded fields on a hillside in Vietnam

Funny Food Faces

When children in Japan open their lunchboxes, they may get to see their favorite animal or cartoon character.

These colorful lunchboxes are called bento boxes.

Japanese moms turn food into animal faces, superheroes, cars, flowers, and many other shapes.

A bento box

The main food in a bento box is usually rice balls. The **ingredients** used to make the meal might also include seaweed, mini hot dogs, salmon, omelettes or hard-boiled eggs, cubes of cheese, **pickled** vegetables, and fruit.

Animal faces made from rice balls, sliced hot dogs, and seaweed

Homemade Diwali Sweets

Diwali is a **festival** that celebrates the victory of light over darkness and of good over evil.

It is also known as the festival of lights.

Hindu, Sikh, and Jain people all over the world celebrate Diwali.

People eat lots of homemade sweets and give sweets as gifts.

They light fireworks and decorate their homes with small oil lamps.

Diwali sweets are made from many ingredients, including flour, beans, lentils, carrots, pumpkins, nuts, raisins, and yogurt. Sweet **spices** such as cinnamon and nutmeg are also used.

Hunting and Gathering

The Baka are a group of people who live in **rain forests** in Africa.

They are **hunter-gatherers** who get their food from the forest.

Baka men hunt for antelopes, crocodiles, and monkeys.

Women and children catch fish, turtles, termites, caterpillars, and giant land snails to eat.

A giant land snail

Baka people find mushrooms and berries in the forest. They also search for beehives in trees. Then they gather the honey to eat.

Yak Meat and Milk

In Tibet, people raise hairy cattle called yaks.

Yak farmers get meat and milk from their animals.

Yak butter for sale in a market

Drying yak dung

People collect yak dung, or poop.

Then they dry the dung and burn it as fuel for cooking and heating.

Tibetan people make butter from yak milk. The butter is mixed with water, tea, and salt to make butter tea. This warming, fatty tea is the favorite drink of people in Tibet.

A yak pulling a sled loaded with hay to feed the yak herd

A Fish Supper

In the United Kingdom, many people love to eat fish and chips.

It's **traditional** to have this food for supper on a Friday night, or at the seaside, or shore.

Most towns in the UK have a fish and chips shop.

People eat lots of extras with fish and chips such as mushy peas, pickles, pickled onions, gravy, and even curry sauce.

A supper of fish and chips at the shore

Together for Iftar

For Muslims, Ramadan is the holiest month of the year. During this time, adults and teenagers fast, or don't eat, between sunrise and sunset.

Children sometimes fast for just half the day.

Each evening, after sunset, families and friends gather for a special evening meal called *iftar*.

Many people break, or stop, their fast each evening by eating fruit called dates.

A family eating iftar in Indonesia

An iftar meal in the United Arab Emirates

Ramadan is when God, or Allah, first revealed parts of Islam's holy book, the Quran (kuh-RAN). During Ramadan, Muslims say extra prayers, fast, and try to give up bad habits. Fasting is a way to show their faith in Allah. It also helps people remember that not everyone has enough to eat.

Not Enough Food to Eat

Around the world, many children and their families do not have enough to eat.

Families may be too poor to buy food.

Some people live in places where it is difficult to grow food.

Others live in places where wars keep food from reaching people who need it to survive.

People looking for food in garbage

In Brazil's cities, many children live on the streets. They have no parents or grown-ups to take care of them. They sleep in cardboard boxes and search for food in garbage bins. **Charities** and other helpers try to bring food and drink to the street children.

Street children in Brazil eating

Welcome to My World

GLOSSARY

charity
An organization that raises money and uses it to do good work, such as helping people living in poverty.

festival
A day or several days when a large number of people enjoy a celebration. Most festivals are connected to special times in a religion.

hunter-gatherer
A person who gets most of their food by hunting, fishing, or gathering wild foods.

ingredient
A food or substance that is used to make a particular dish or meal—for example, flour, eggs, and sugar are ingredients used to make a cake.

pickled
Put into vinegar or salty water. Foods such as onions and mini cucumbers are often pickled. This gives them a tangy taste and makes them last for a long time.

plow
To dig up the soil with a large tool that is called a plow. Soil is plowed to make it soft and crumbly and ready for young plants or seeds to be planted. A plow can be pulled over the ground by an animal or a tractor.

rain forest
A thick forest of trees and other plants. More than 13 feet (4 m) of rain falls in a rain forest each year.

spices
Dried parts of plants, such as seeds, that are used as ingredients in cooking. Spices are used to give foods more flavor or different colors.

traditional
Done in a certain way for many years by a group of people—for example, eating a particular type of food.

INDEX

B
Baka people 12–13
bento boxes 8–9
breakfast 4
butter 14–15

D
dinner (supper) 4, 16–17, 18–19
Diwali 10–11

F
fasting 18–19
fish and chips 16–17
fruit 5, 9, 11, 13, 18

G
growing food 5, 6–7, 20

H
Hindu people 10
honey 13
hunger and poverty 20–21
hunting 12

I
iftar 18–19

J
Jain people 10

L
lunch 4, 8–9

M
milk 14–15
Muslim people 18–19

R
rain forests 12–13
Ramadan 18–19
rice 6–7, 8–9

S
Sikh people 10
spices 11
sweets 10–11

V
vegetables 5, 9, 11, 16

Y
yaks 14–15